Death by Laughter

A CARTOON COLLECTION BY HARRY BLISS

INTRODUCTION BY CHRISTOPHER GUEST

ABRAMS IMAGE | NEW YORK

For Harry Bliss

Acknowledgments

Many thanks to Alex Bliss, John Butler, Joanna Cotler,
Carol Dolnick, Kate DiCamillo, Sofi Dillof, Tony Dillof, Mary Elson,
Pat Fitzmaurice, Christopher Guest, Grim Reaper, Sean Knight,
Charlie Kochman, Holly McGhee, Arlene Rosenberg,
Michael Steiner, James Sturm, and Peter Woodward.

Introduction

WHEN I WAS A CHILD, I HAD TWO FANTASIES: The first was to play center field for the New York Yankees. The second was to be a cartoonist.

As it happened, Mickey Mantle was doing quite well, and the possibility of my joining the team seemed increasingly remote. Therefore, my ball playing was limited to the playgrounds of Greenwich Village. Not the number-one recruiting area in the nation, it turned out.

But I could still draw—on every surface of every school notebook, every shirt cardboard my dad got back from the laundry. My proud parents framed many of them, leading me to believe that my future was secure. I was twelve, but certainly the *New Yorker* would be calling any day now.

There was a problem, however. I could only draw characters facing in one direction. And there were no captions. No actual jokes or even humorous situations. Just people facing left, sometimes holding a book under their arm. By the time I was fifty, I stopped waiting for calls from the *New Yorker*. Mind you, I had never submitted any drawings to them, so the logic was a bit fuzzy.

Today, I have found other means of employment, but my love of cartoons is still deep. My wife and I have been collecting originals for more than twenty years. We have a gallery of the Greats, and among them is the work of Harry Bliss.

Harry has created a collection of work that is extraordinary. Laugh-out-loud funny, dark, surreal, and socially stinging. His characters (which face both directions, incidentally) are dogs, accountants, doctors, and Death. All inhabit a world that is familiar but somehow slightly off. Bliss's range is remarkable. From the understated elegance of his black-and-white cartoons to the dazzling paintings that grace the covers of the *New Yorker* magazine, his is a unique blend of domestic observation and impending doom. His work seems so on target that one feels there is no hiding from the truth.

Harry Bliss is brilliantly talented and prolific, and I am honored to be able to introduce his book.

—Christopher Guest

CHRISTOPHER GUEST is known for having written, directed, and starred in several films, including *This is Spinal Tap*, *Waiting for Guffman*, and *Best in Show*.

*"It's almost like we've died and gone to he—
wait a minute . . . We're dead!"*

"I'd invite you up . . . but I'm pretty sure we
both know what that would lead to."

"*Oh, that's just great.* Now *you want to reach out to us!*"

"You can just say you don't like it . . . You don't have to make that face!"

"... Hold on ... I think a table's about to open up ..."

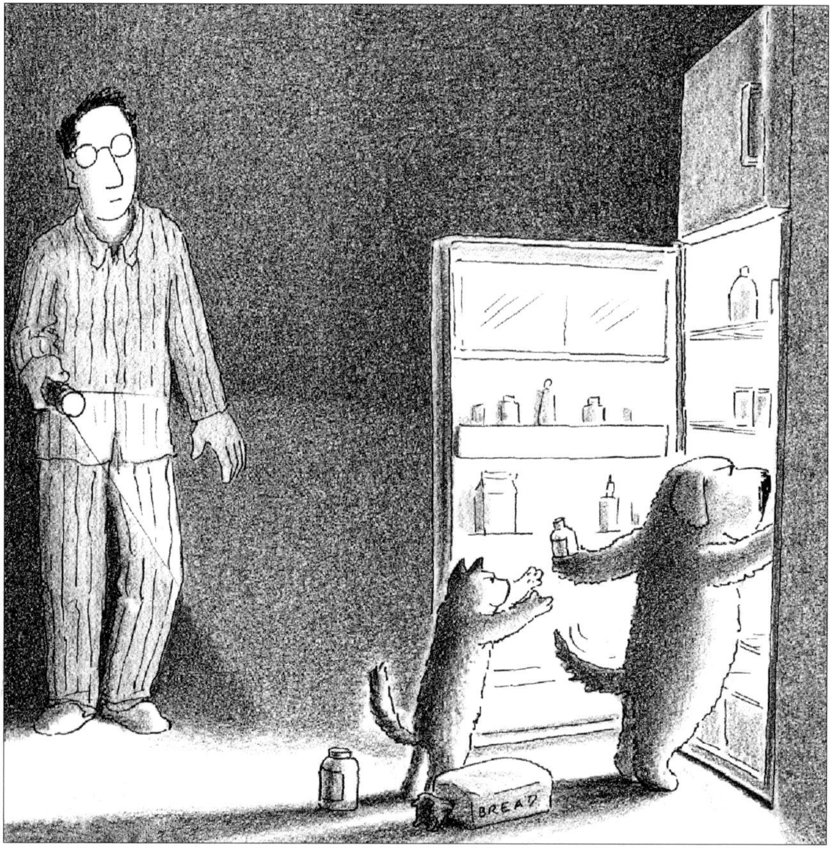
BREAD

"That one's a mistake."

"Someday, Son, all this *will be yours . . . Sorry."*

"Wow. From way up here you can really get a good look at the hole in the ozone layer."

"OK, Alanis . . . Let's try it one more time with a little less feeling."

LOOKING FOR THAT SPECIAL SOMEONE. MUST BE BOLD, ADVENTURESOME, AND NOT AFRAID TO FACE THEIR GREATEST FEARS.

"Owww!! Yes, that hurts!"

"Just let me finish working on this cure for cancer.
Then, Doctor Skylar, I'll pull your finger."

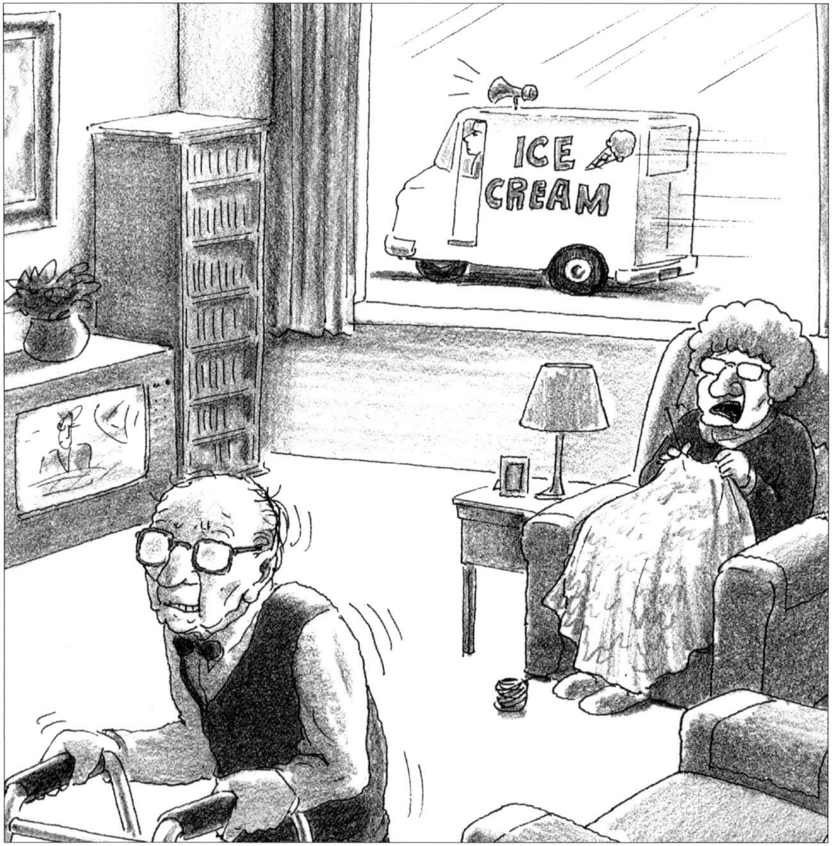
ICE CREAM

"You'll never make it!"

"*I still reap . . . I just got tired of being grim.*"

*"With the benefit of hindsight, do you feel it was
wise to dedicate your first children's book to Hitler?"*

"... I promised myself I wouldn't do this ..."

"*I* knew *it!*"

"I still cannot believe catnip is legal."

"I'm, like, totally not even helping."

"Whaddaya say we skip the Johnsons' house?
Grandpa's on a tight schedule."

"Could you pass the peanuts?"

"I met him at Costco."

"This is so *much better than the couch!"*

"Ladies and gentlemen, this is your captain speaking.
Sorry about the turbulence . . . The co-pilot and I thought it
might be fun to fly upside down."

"Can you hear me now?"

"Honey, I've found God!"

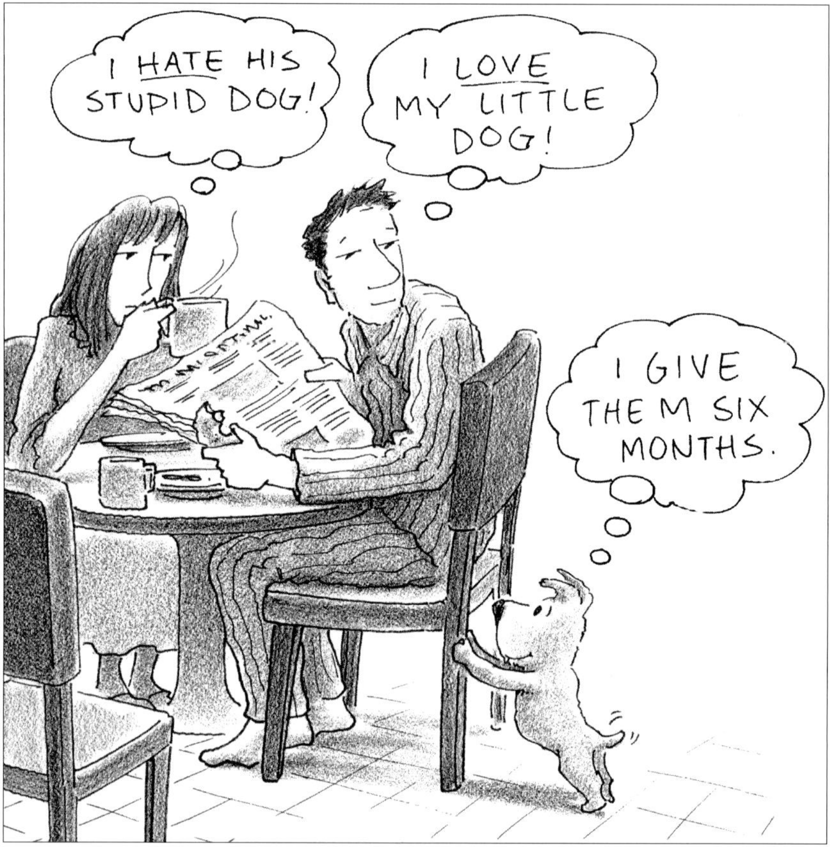
I HATE HIS STUPID DOG!
I LOVE MY LITTLE DOG!
I GIVE THEM SIX MONTHS.

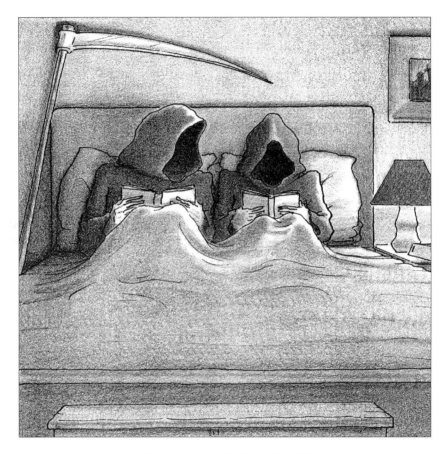

"Did you lock the front door?"

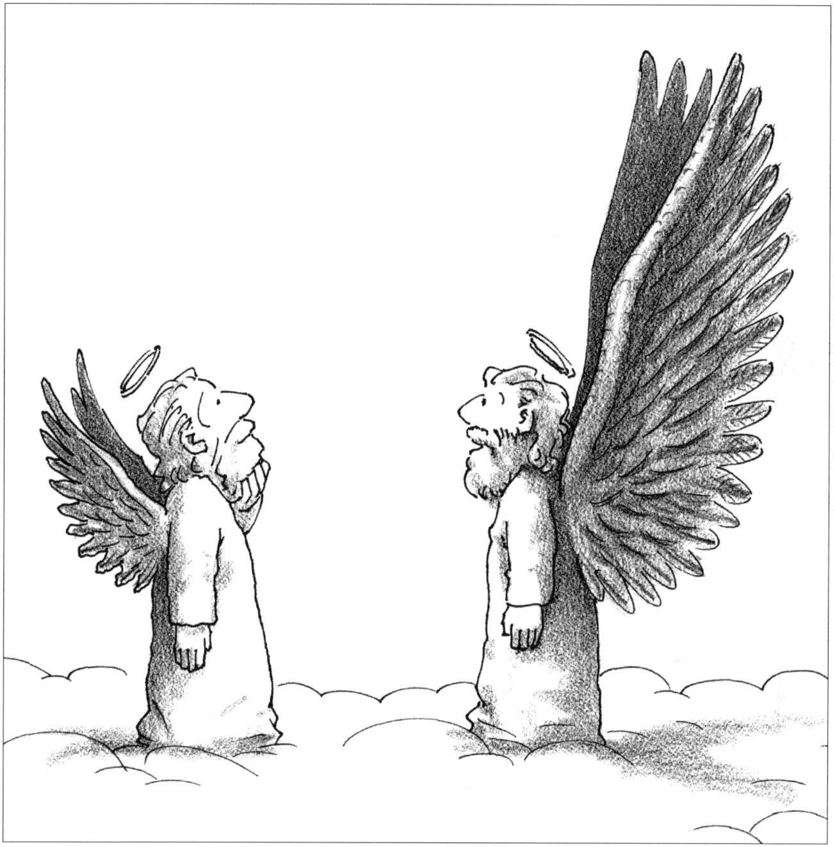

"eBay."

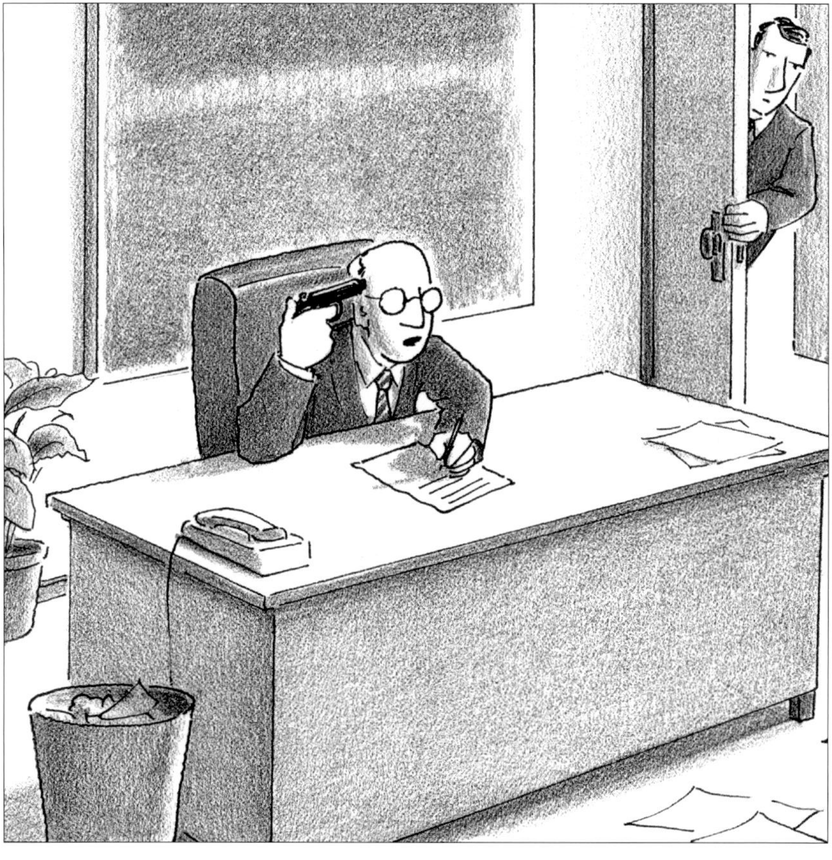

"Can it wait?"

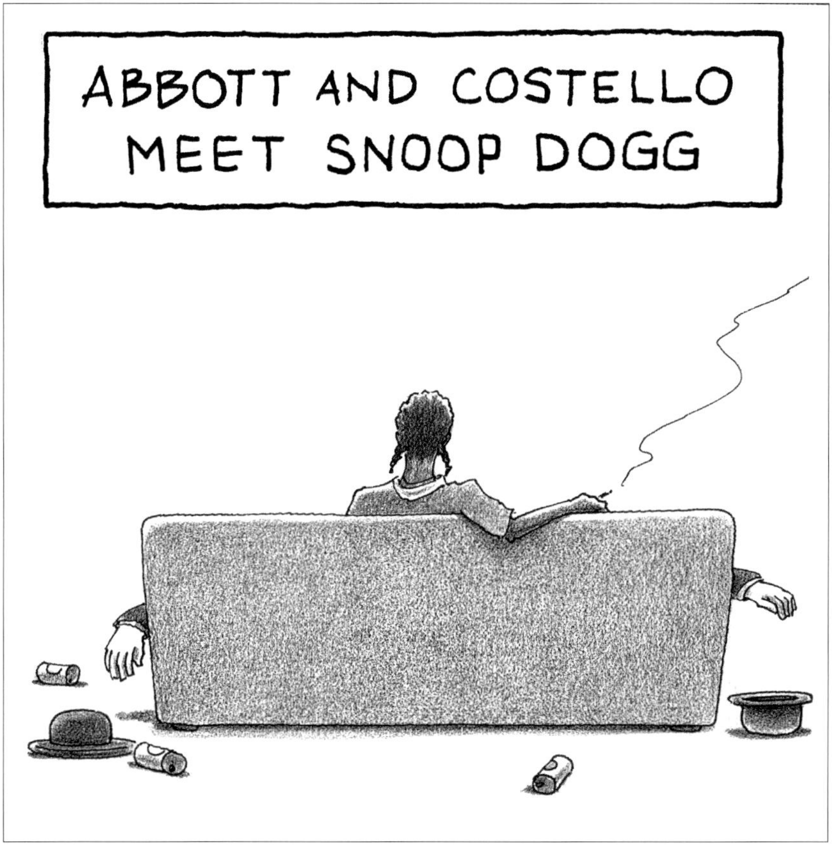
ABBOTT AND COSTELLO
MEET SNOOP DOGG

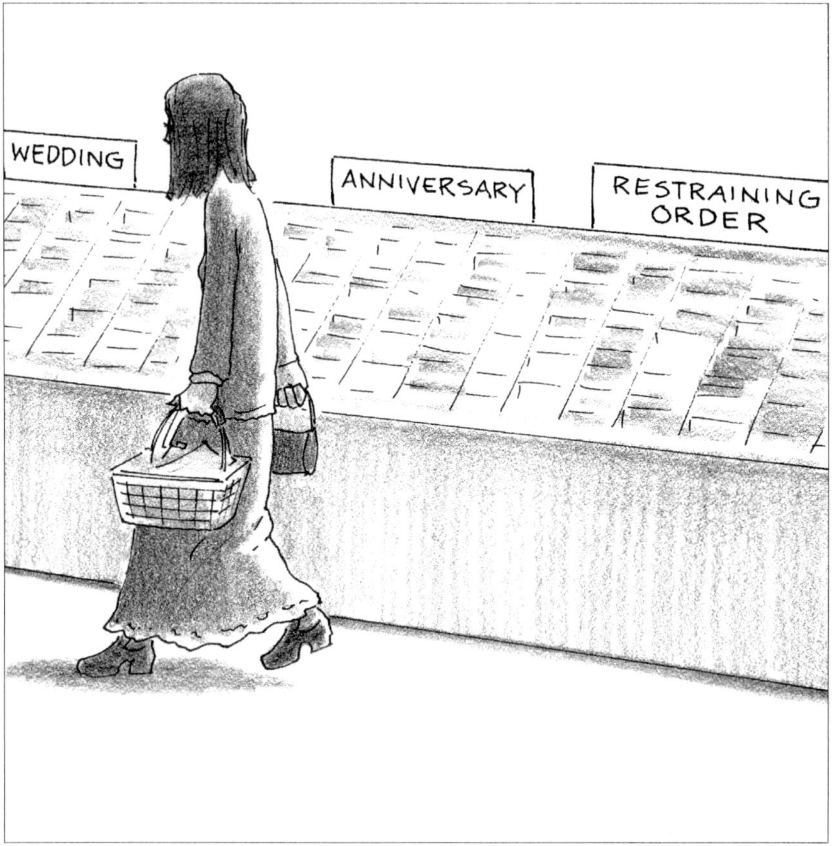
WEDDING
ANNIVERSARY
RESTRAINING ORDER

*"Do you ever worry about being left for dead
in the middle of nowhere by someone you trust?"*

"Housekeeping!"

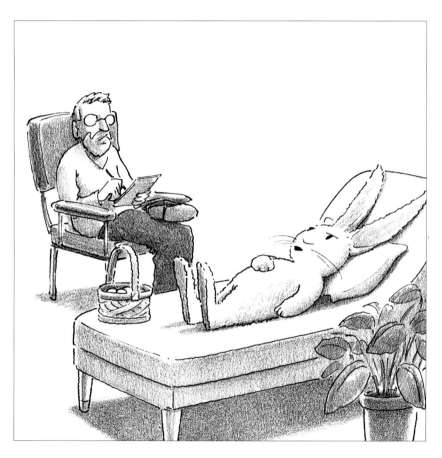

"... I dunno, I guess I just don't believe in myself anymore."

"That's it, Mister . . . You just lost your 'free range' status!"

"Well, if it isn't Ulysses finally back from the Trojan War!"

"*Your grandfather just paid off his student loan.*"

"When I turn ninety, I am so experimenting with drugs."

"*You must be the artist.*"

"So, Owen tells me you guys met in art school."

"No, Barbara, this wouldn't make a 'great Seinfeld episode'!"

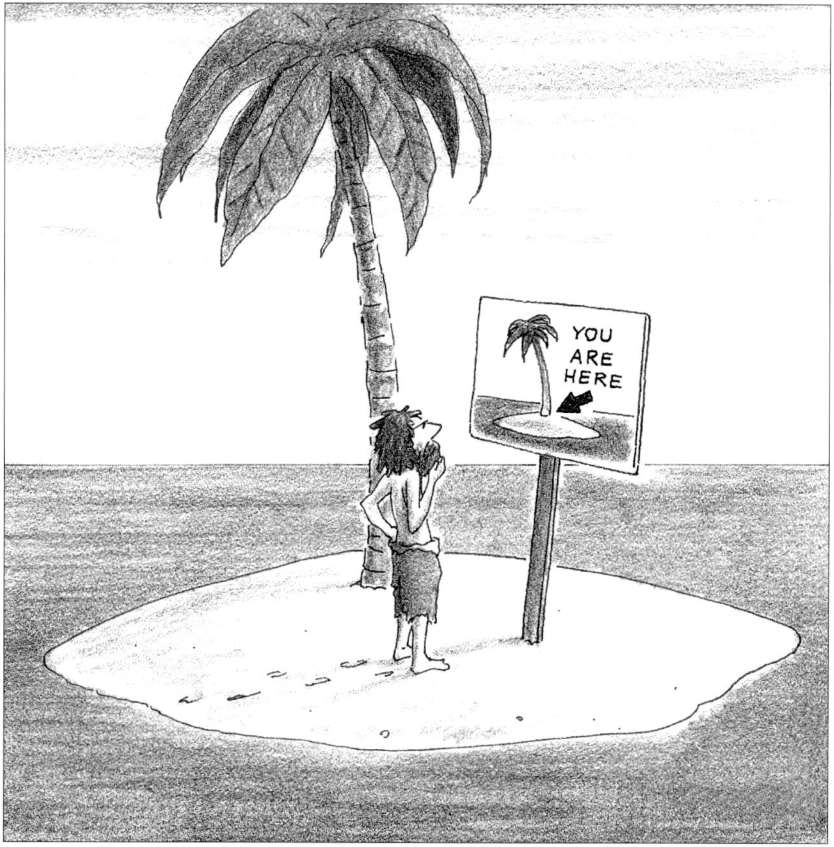
YOU
ARE
HERE

"... Most of all ... I miss the way you scratched my butt."

"Well, whaddaya know—my old childhood drugs!"

"Part of me wants to blame everything on my parents—
but it's the same part of me that sucked the life out of them."

*"Let me call you back, Carol—the creepy guy
I married keeps checking me out."*

"Does her dress make me look fat?"

"See this area right here? That's where you
have that stupid song stuck in your head."

"My God, you're right . . . It all makes sense:
I crossed the road because of my parents!"

"Look, Son—Pop-Pop and Nana are heading south for the winter."

"Oh my God, Mother! That is, like, so passive-aggressive!"

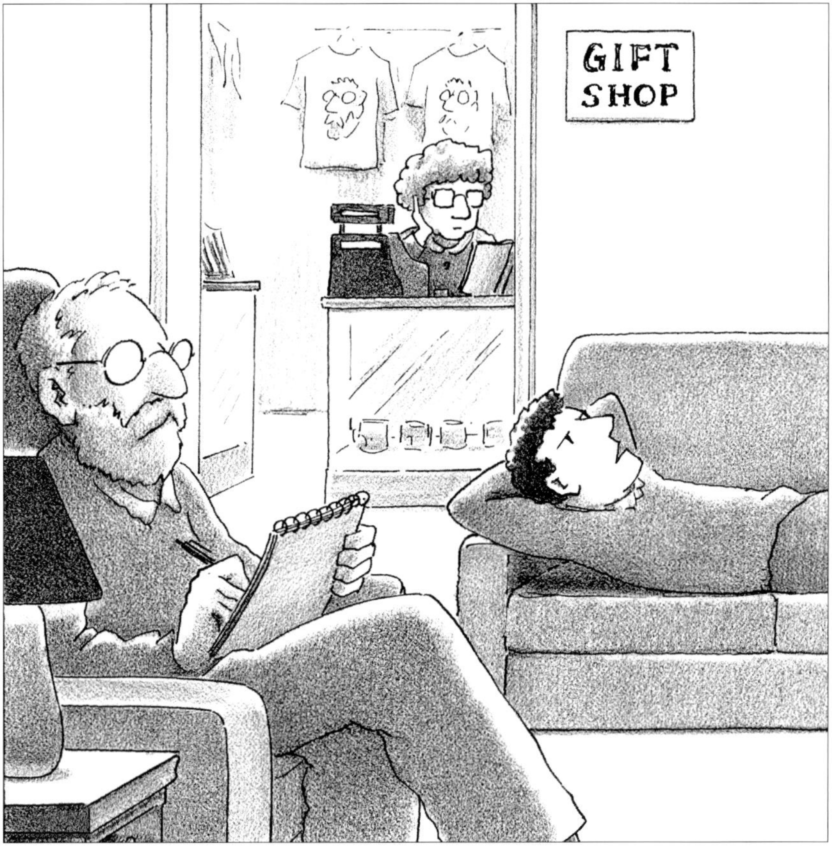
GIFT
SHOP

"*Relax, boy. That's just God.*"

"He came with Grandma."

"Tom, I'd like you to meet Chris—Chris is better than you."

*"We'd like a quiet table for two where my wife
can justify spending three grand on a handbag."*

"I'd invite you in, but my crap is all over the place."

*"The real question is, do we want to give up
all this lake access just to evolve?"*

"Harold, do you hear this? He's marrying a shiksa!"

"*The previous owners had the basement finished
into a terrific 'mother-in-law apartment.*'"

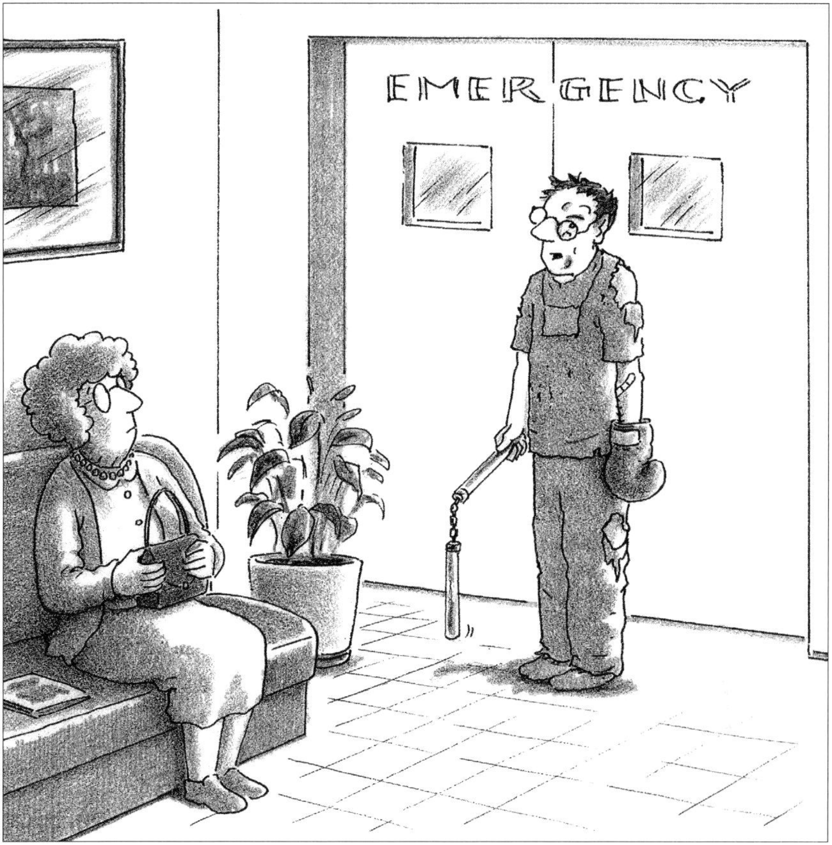
EMERGENCY

"He fought like hell."

"Yes, tech support? My laptop kept freezing up,
so I stabbed it with a knife . . . What do I do now?"

"We're not too concerned about college . . .
Dale and I are pretty sure he's going to prison."

"You're not even listening, are you?!"

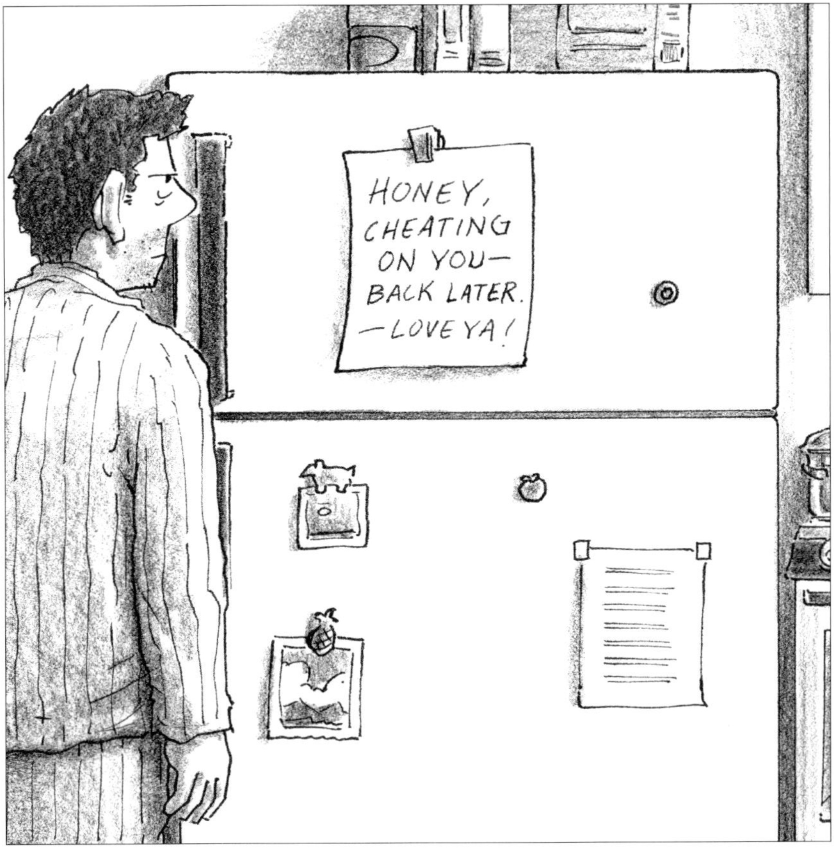
HONEY, CHEATING ON YOU— BACK LATER. —LOVE YA!

"Looks like the hypochondria finally got him."

"Doctor, enough with the 'clear.' My husband's dead!"

"Joe, toilet water for everyone . . . The bitch said 'yes!'"

"I hate to break it to you, but you weren't his best friend."

PUPPY-INFESTED
WATERS

"Isn't this nice? No snow, no traffic . . . just you, me, and the ocean."

"... I guess you had to be there."

". . . All the lab work confirms it—I'm sorry, Mr. Franklin . . . You're old."

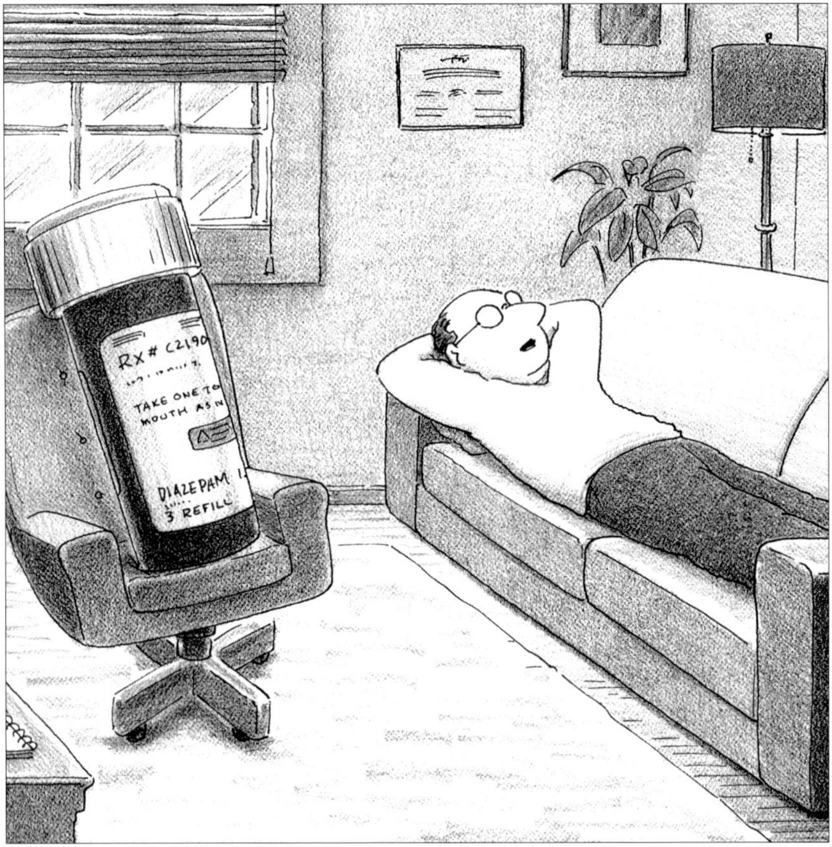
RX # C2190
TAKE ONE TO
MOUTH AS
DIAZEPAM
3 REFILL

"I knew you'd *understand."*

"I feel bad . . . We only call our coke dealer when we need something."

"*Here I am, Mother, gainfully and meaningfully employed, and all you can do is criticize.*"

"Mom, Dad, I'm gay. Damn, that was easy."

". . . and her thighs kept getting bigger and bigger . . ."

*"So, if I give the ol' man one of my kidneys,
about how long before I can expect it back?"*

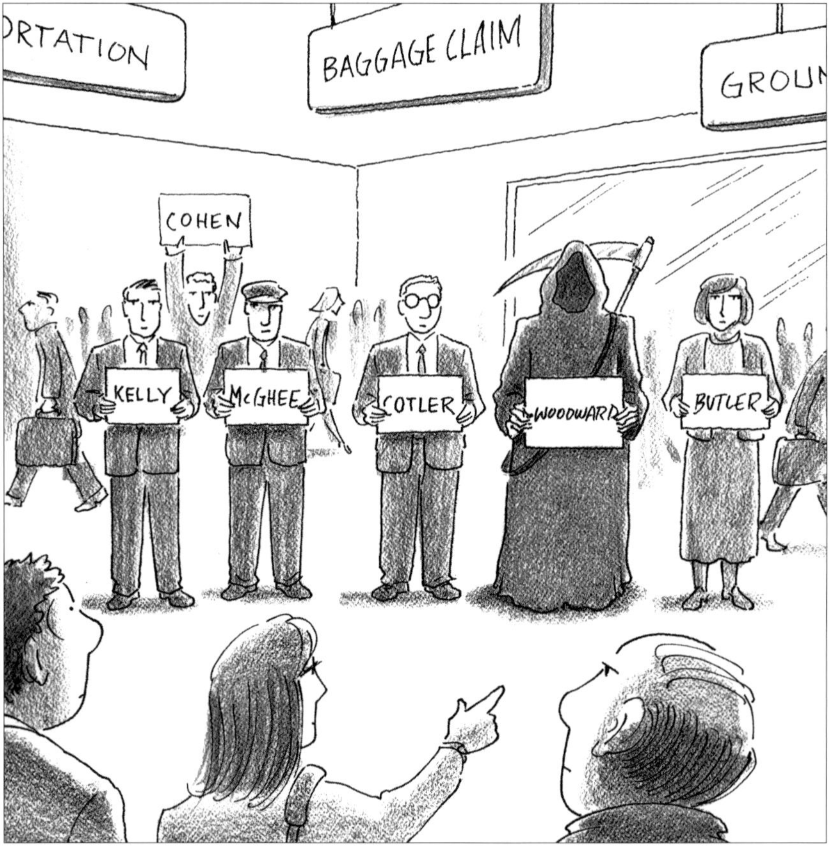
RTATION
BAGGAGE CLAIM
GROUN
COHEN
KELLY
McGHEE
COTLER
WOODWARD
BUTLER

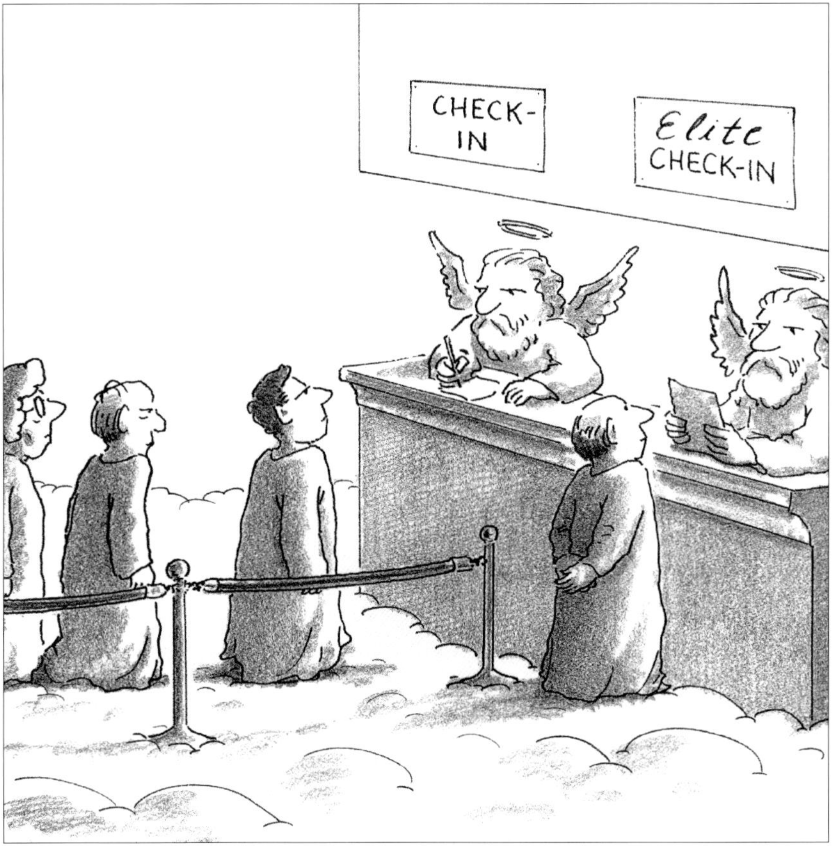
CHECK-
IN
Elite
CHECK-IN

"My client would like to remind the senator from Pennsylvania and the rest of the Judiciary Committee members that she's just a little puppy."

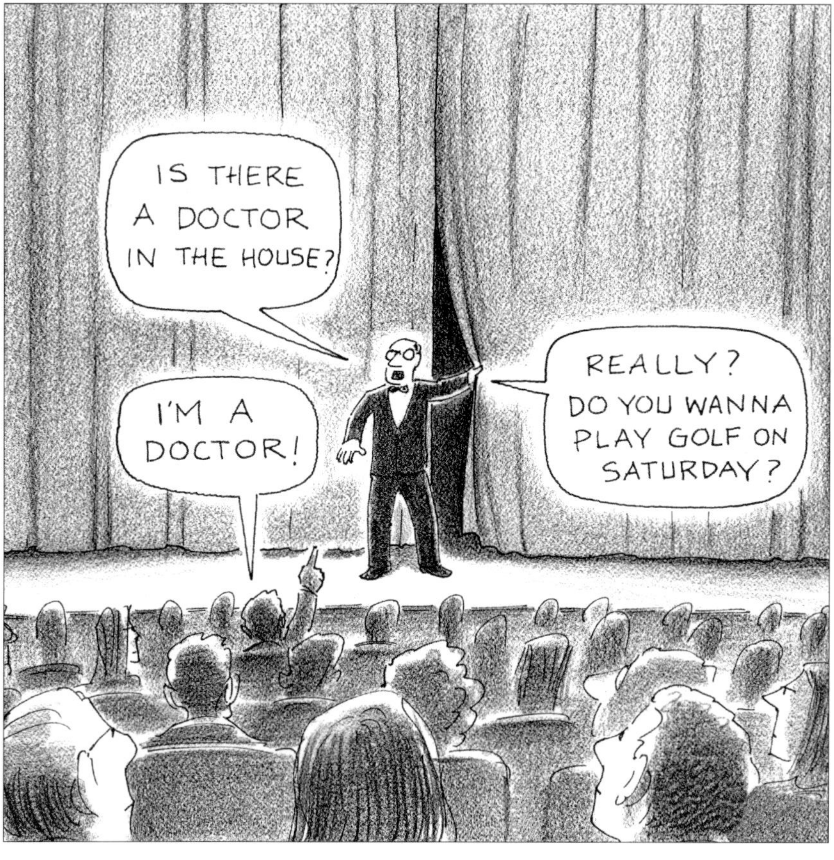
IS THERE A DOCTOR IN THE HOUSE?
I'M A DOCTOR!
REALLY? DO YOU WANNA PLAY GOLF ON SATURDAY?

"Can you recommend a nice red wine that goes well with a broken heart?"

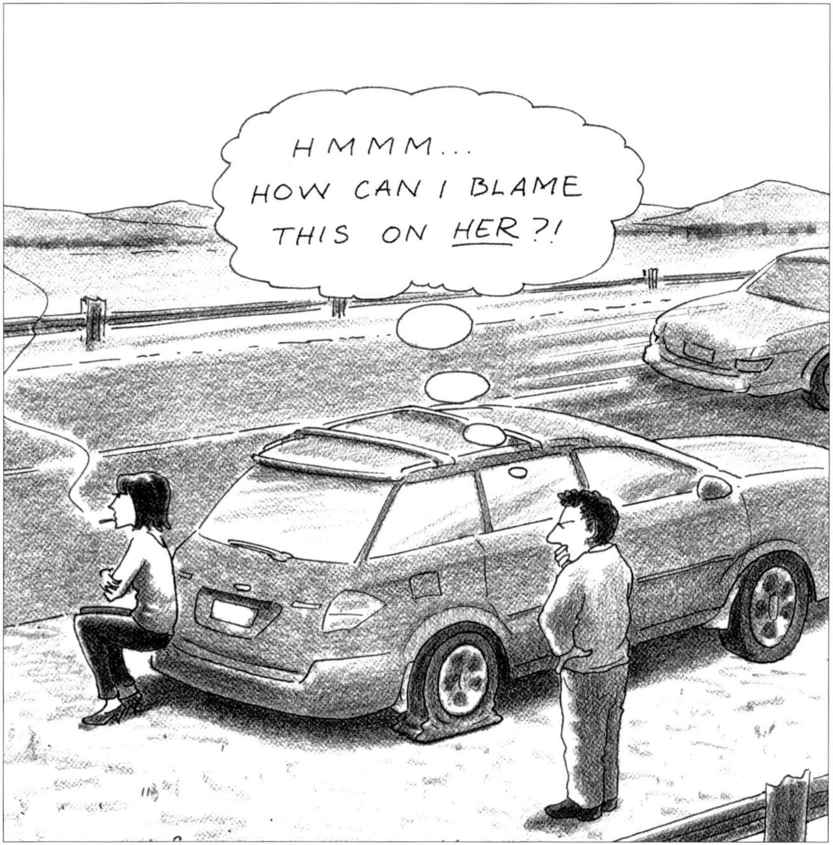
HMMM...
HOW CAN I BLAME
THIS ON HER?!

"*Quit complaining. I let you keep your hair.*"

"I know how much you hated *my meatloaf."*

"Tom, quick—check it out. This virus looks just like your wife's tattoo."

"Is that a new look of disgust you're wearing?"

"Well, for starters, you're holding the shovel all wrong."

"Honey, wake up! He's doing it again!"

"Listen, Mom, I gotta go. There's a telemarketer on the other line."

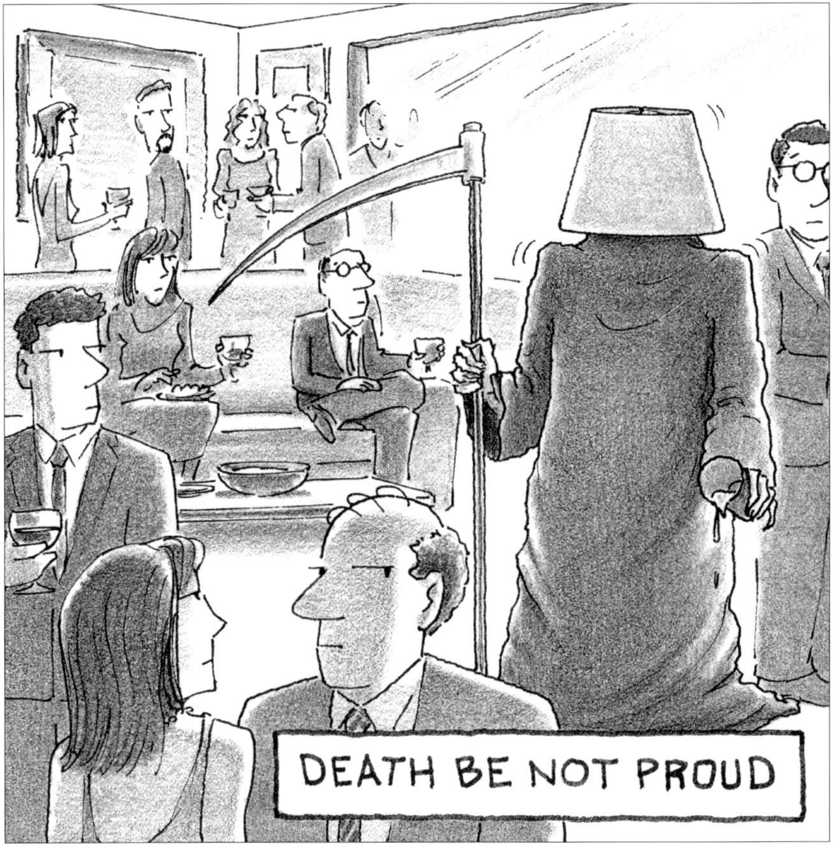
DEATH BE NOT PROUD

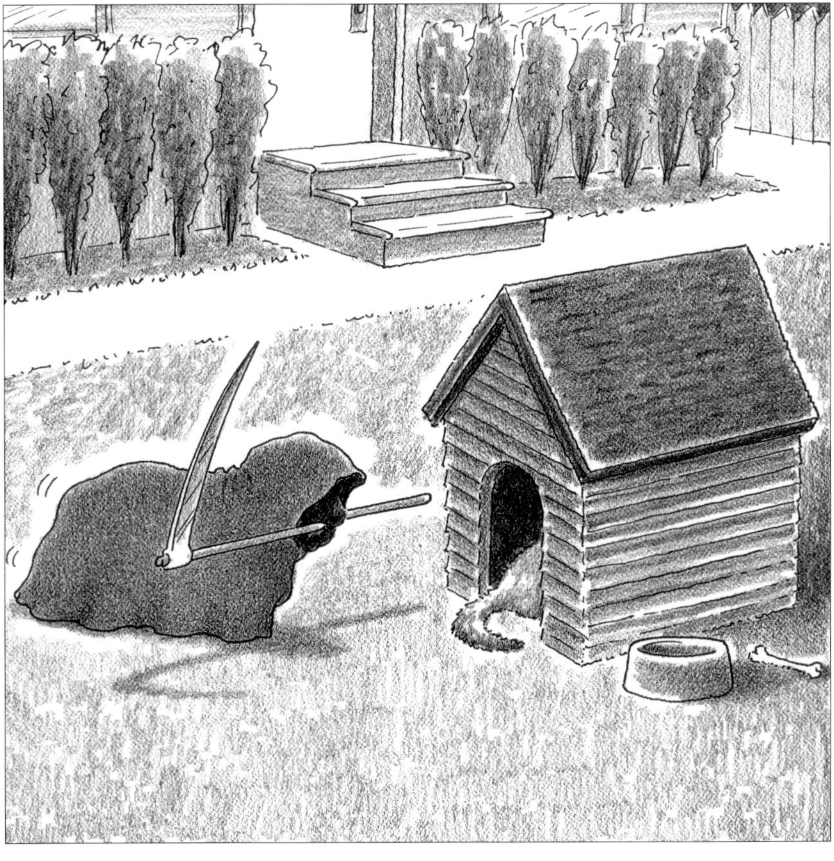

"Let's see . . . We'll take Death."

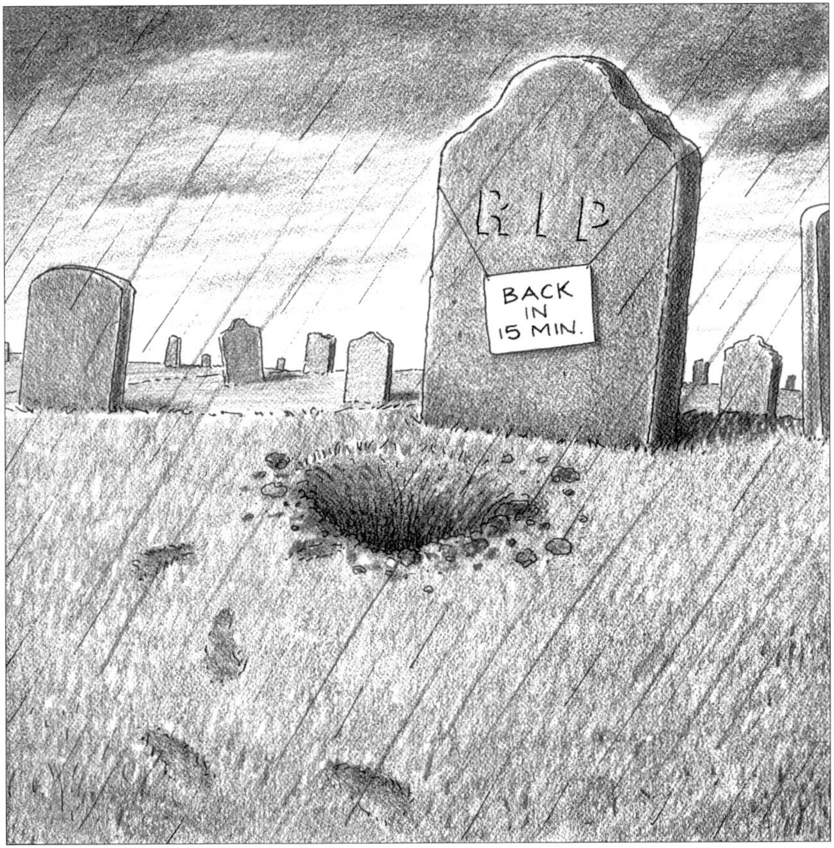
RIP
BACK
IN
15 MIN.

AROMAPSYCHOTHERAPY

"'Peacefully in his sleep' my ass.*"*

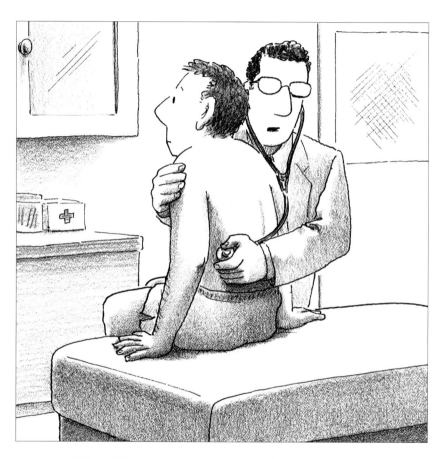

"How did you get your heart to stop beating like that?"

... 'He is survived by his wife and three children.' Hmmm,
no mention of your 'best friend.'"

"I'm, like, totally not even guarding anything."

"If you folks can give me a couple of minutes,
I do believe a table's opening up."

"Can you hear me calling you an idiot now?!"

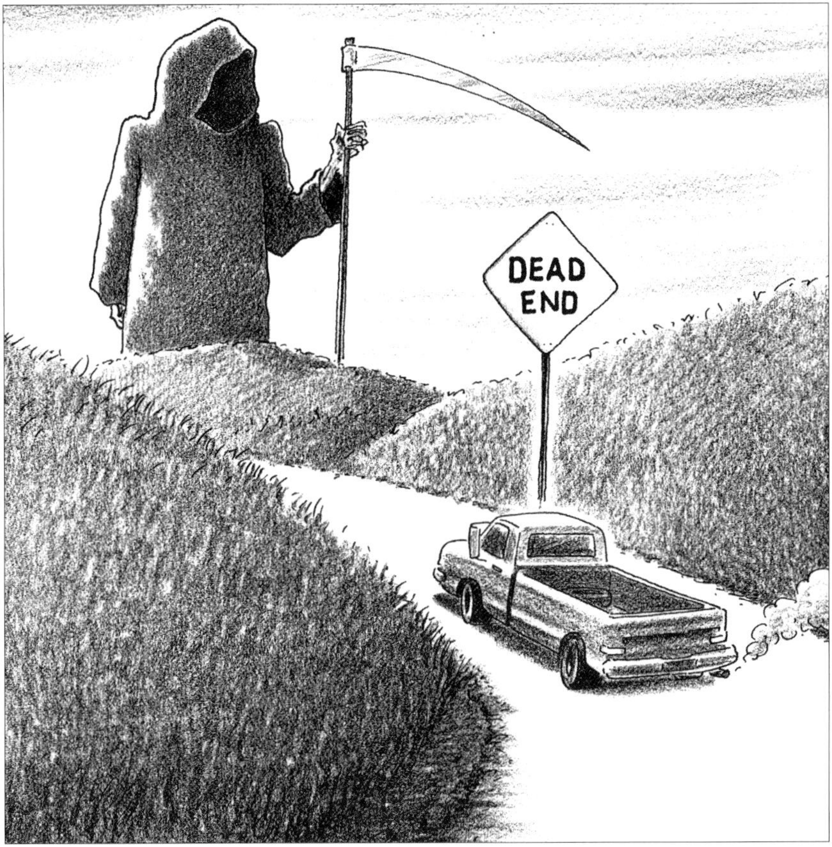
DEAD
END

"*Hey, it's me. I'll be there in, like, twenty minutes.
I just have this one last person to kill.*"

"Let me call you back, Ed. I'm about to get mugged."

"How about that—did that hurt?"

"OK, I know that this is borderline inappropriate,
but just hear me out . . ."

*"You're doing that thing again where you're
my husband and you're next to me in bed."*

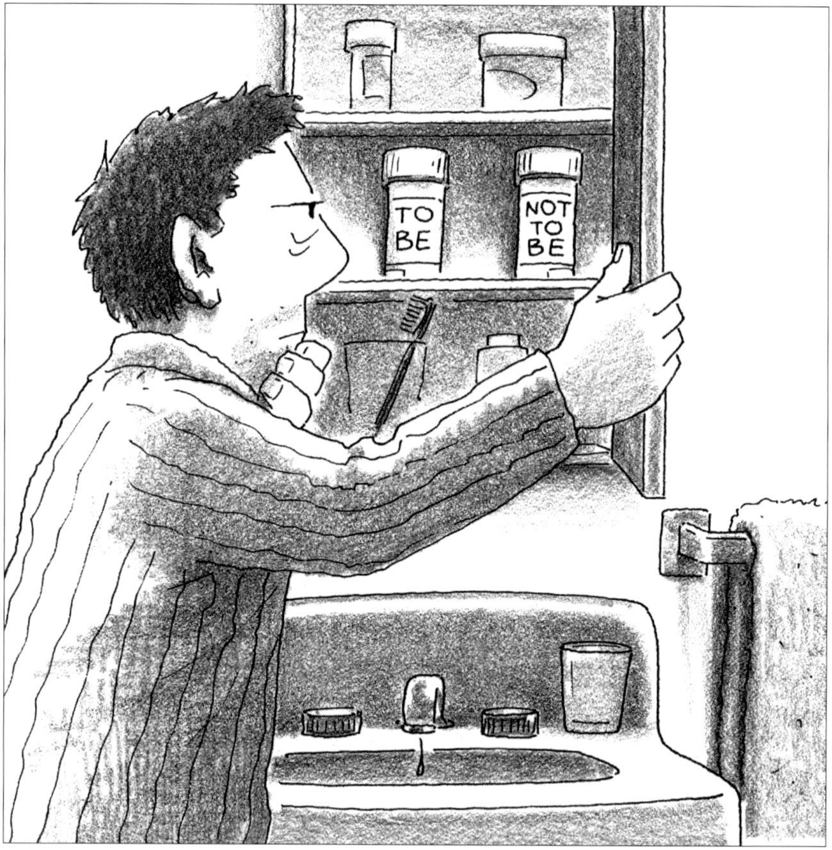
TO
BE
NOT
TO
BE

"Look, we've gone over this a million times—
I'm just not ready to meet your parents."

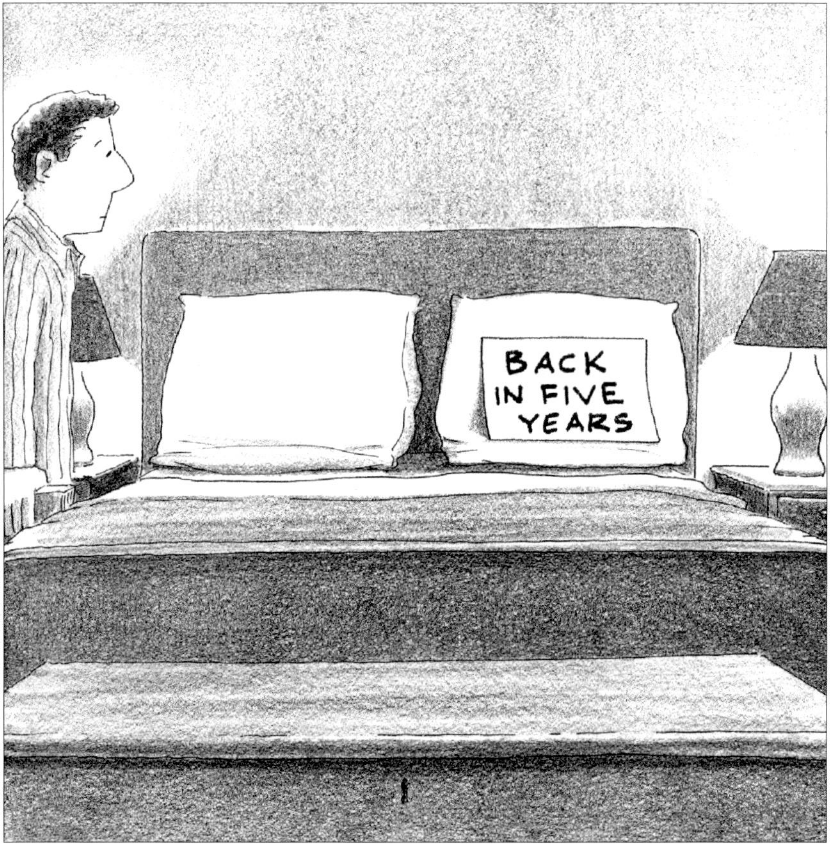
BACK IN FIVE YEARS

"*Remember that time you tried to kill me?*"

"What took you so long?"

"Hold on, it may not *be over . . . There's a fatter lady over there."*

Editor: Charles Kochman
Editorial Assistant: Sofia Gutiérrez
Designer: Nancy Leonard
Production Manager: Jacqueline Poirer

Library of Congress Cataloging-in-Publication Data

Bliss, Harry, 1964-
Death by laughter : written and illustrated by Harry Bliss ; introduction by Christopher Guest.
p. cm.
ISBN 978-0-8109-7084-7
1. Death–Caricatures and cartoons. 2. American wit and humor, Pictorial.
I. Guest, Christopher. II. Title.

NC1429.B623A4 2008
741.5'6973–dc22

2007029641

Published in 2008 by Abrams Image, an imprint of Harry N. Abrams, Inc.

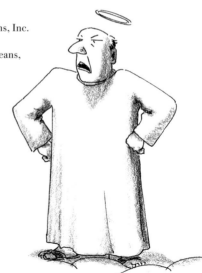

Printed and bound in China.
10 9 8 7 6 5 4 3 2 1

HNA
harry n. abrams, inc.
a subsidiary of La Martinière Groupe

115 West 18th Street
New York, NY 10011
www.hnabooks.com